Polly Pocket

by Julie Murray

Abdo Kids Jumbo is an Imprint of Abdo Kids
abdobooks.com

abdobooks.com

Published by Abdo Kids, a division of ABDO, P.O. Box 398166, Minneapolis, Minnesota 55439.

Printed in the United States of America, North Mankato, Minnesota.

102025

012026

Photo Credits: AP Images, Getty Images, Shutterstock,
©The Strong National Museum of Play, Rochester, New York, p.cover

Production Contributors: Teddy Borth, Jennie Forsberg, Grace Hansen
Design Contributors: Candice Keimig, Pakou Moua

Library of Congress Control Number: 2025936484

Publisher's Cataloging-in-Publication Data

Names: Murray, Julie, author.

Title: Polly Pocket / by Julie Murray

Description: Minneapolis, Minnesota : Abdo Kids, 2026 | Series: Toy mania! | Includes online resources and index.

Identifiers: ISBN 9798384907596 (lib. bdg.) | ISBN 9798384908296 (ebook) | ISBN 9798384908647 (read-to-me ebook)

Subjects: LCSH: Polly Pocket dolls--Juvenile literature. | Dolls--Juvenile literature. | Character dolls—Juvenile literature. | Hasbro Entertainment (Firm)--Juvenile literature. | Toys--Juvenile literature. | Toys--History--Juvenile literature.

Classification: DDC 688.7221--dc23

Table of Contents

Polly Pocket

Polly Pocket is a toy line of mini dolls and playsets. The tiny toys spark big imagination. For more than 35 years, Polly Pocket has delighted kids!

Inspiration

In 1983, Chris Wiggs came up with the idea for Polly Pocket. He was **inspired** by a makeup **compact**. He used this to create a mini doll and dollhouse for his daughter.

Wiggs wanted the toy to be small enough to fit into someone's pocket. The name Polly Pocket was born! Kids could easily take the toy with them anywhere.

The tiny Polly Pocket dolls were less than 1 inch (2.5 cm) tall. They had a round base that fit into holes inside the case. The dolls also folded in the middle. The case could close with every **accessory** inside.

Wiggs worked with Bluebird Toys to get his creation into stores. The first playsets **debuted** in 1989. Polly Pocket became very popular.

Bluebird
Polly Pocket
THE POCKET-SIZED PLAYMATE YOU CAN TAKE ANYWHERE
POLLY'S CAFÉ
CAFE
PLAY WITH IT ON ITS OWN OR WITH OTHER GREAT COLLECTABLES, ALL FROM POLLY POCKET'S TINY WORLD
Bluebird®
BLUEBIRD TOYS P.L.C.
SWINDON, ENGLAND
©1989
MADE IN CHINA

Fresh Design

Mattel bought the Polly Pocket brand in 1998. The company **debuted** the Fashion Polly line in 1999. The new dolls were bigger. They came with rubbery clothes that could be changed.

kable Studios
Game Room
polly
pocket™
WARNING:
CHOKING HAZARD – Small parts
Not for children under 3 years.
4+
Stackable Studios
Crissy® Beach Room

Later, Polly Pocket became less popular. The toy line went away in 2012. But, in 2018, Mattel decided to bring back the mini cases that kids loved so much!

Today’s Polly Pocket dolls are a bit bigger than the original. They are made of a special plastic that helps them stand on their own. Their bodies bend so they can be placed in different positions.

WARNING:
CHOKING HAZARD – Small parts.
Not for children under 3 years.
ATTENTION :
DANGER D'ÉTOUFFEMENT –
Petits éléments. Ne convient pas
aux enfants de moins de 36 mois.
POLLY STICK
POLLY STICK
Polly Pocket
4+
ADVERTENCIA:
PELIGRO DE ASFIXIA. Juguete no recomendado para
menores de 3 años. Contiene piezas pequeñas que podrían
provocar asfixia en caso de ser ingeridas por el niño/a.
19

Over the years, TV shows and movies **featuring** Polly Pocket have been made. New playsets and dolls have been created too. Today, Polly Pocket continues to offer lots of fun in a little case!

Polly
Pocket
TINY IS MIGHTY!™

More Facts

- The original Polly Pocket cases were shaped like shells, hearts, and circles. The line grew to include campers, castles, and more!

- Bluebird Toys **debuted** the Mighty Max toy line in 1992. The toys had tiny dolls and cases, just like Polly Pocket. But the cases came in spooky shapes, like snakes and skulls!

- Polly Pocket was **inducted** into the National Toy Hall of Fame in 2004.

Glossary

accessory – an item added on to something to make it prettier or more complete.

compact – a small case that contains makeup and a mirror.

debuted – presented for the first time.

featuring – including as an important part.

inducted – brought in as a member.

inspired – given a new idea by something.

Index

Visit **abdokids.com** to access crafts, games, videos, and more!

Use Abdo Kids code

TPK7596

or scan this QR code!